First published in the United Kingdom 2023 by LifeZone

Copyright © LifeZone Publishing ® , Parkhurst,

Johannesburg, RSA

My Animals and Other Families

Introduction:

This book of illustrated poems has been created as a satirical work, aimed at the younger generation in an effort to amuse, and educate. The poems are anthropomorphic and contrast the human characteristics of people we all know and love, with our animal friends. Animals have an innate ability to display their sense of family bonds, but where they do not, we can still recognise those elements of our own families in their behaviour.

Each poem has been written to provide a sense of those familiar characters in our families and schools, with whom we can see the resemblance to animals. Although domesticated animals, like dogs, or cats have the most humanistic of characteristics, I have chosen to compare non-domesticated, and wild animals for the purpose of educating our children.

The poems bring humour and insight to a somewhat mundane way of life, with the intention of reflecting what the original Gerald Durrell books were intended to convey; but in a reverse manner. My Animals and other Families is written in the spirit of the great Durrell anecdotes and his early commentary on how he viewed his family, in light of the animals he chose to become more familiar with.

Contents

Barry the Badger

Barry the Badger is strong and tough,
And you don't want to get in his way,
His claws are like a schoolboy's hands,
When he comes home after play!

Looking like he's been in a rugby scrum,
He seems tattered and torn and rough.
With a scruffy coat of grey and black,
You would think that quite enough!

But he's always happy to dig in the dirt,
Getting filthy as he rolls on the ground,
Like a rugby player rucking in the mud,
He likes to scrummage around!

His feet are covered in spikey hair,
Which protects him from any scratches,
But smells like a rugby player's socks.
After playing lengthy matches!

His legs are like a rugby front row,
Made for pushing when in the mood,
As he heaves and hauls fallen trees,
To search the ground for his food!

Like a player who eats a lot of grub,
They will find when out and about,
But it's not the food you might like,
Of that I'm sure there's no doubt!

For out in the woods he is very happy,
When looking for the tastiest dish,
He likes to eat all creepy crawlies,
And I bet that's not your wish!

Berta the Beaver

Berta the Beaver is a busy old soul,
She is happy in the forest in her familiar role,
No other animal can forage for her food,
When trying so hard for the good of her brood.

Her large front teeth are too big for her face,
As she spends her time chewing at a furious pace,
'Cause Berta the Beaver will never let you down,
Chomping away with a happy frown.

With those sharp teeth she's always working,
And Berta the Beaver is never to be found shirking,
Whilst chopping down all those forest trees,
You would think for her, life's such a breeze.

Down on the water she's right at home,
'Cause Beavers like to make a big log dome,
Building her hutch where the fast streams flow,
Berta the Beaver is always on the go.

She spends all day forming a log jam,
Weaving the branches in a woven dam,
Berta the Beaver never seems that fussed,
Safely knowing that her home won't bust.

You see, Berta the Beaver protects the land,
For which she is never short of lending a hand,
With all that hard work she often delivers,
By stemming the flow of fast flowing rivers.

As Berta the Beaver is a lot like your Mother,
'Cause Beavers are always helping one another,
For it seems she will never rest that easy,
So life for you can be easy-peasy!

Cecil the Swan

Ever so handsome, Cecil swans around,
Down by the Thames on familiar ground,
Our leading man filled with air and grace,
Never a feather will be found out of place.

Cecil the Swan is as likely to be spotted,
At the lake where the Serpentine's dotted,
With all his chums at the club he belongs,
Hollering and hooting their regular songs.

'Cause Cecil is one of the exceptional class,
Whose job in the main is to act like a 'farce',
A Swan who's superior will unlikely refrain,
To stick out his neck and show his disdain.

When Cecil the Swan will attempt to block,
Most other birds he considers inferior flock,
He will squabble over what food's to be had,
And generally behaves in a way that is bad!

He'll swagger around when walking the floor,
If waddling up to those he wants to implore,
Cecil tends to spend far too long over lunch,
And likely thinks he's the pick of the bunch.

'Cause Cecil the Swan is one of those gentry,
Who won't allow other birds access to entry,
Swans of this feather, tend to stick together,
Protecting each other, in all kinds of weather.

But Cecil the Swan is not really that naughty,
Despite showing off and looking so haughty,
Swans really are only creatures of behaviour,
Ingrained by entitlement, breeding and favour!

Cheery Cheetah

Are you that lonely Cheetah,
Out on that grassy track?
Are you inspired to run that race,
And never once look back?

If this is you and you can see,
The goal that you have sought.
Then you my friend will never stop,
Before that prize is caught!

So when you're on that track of Life,
And the sun is high.
Don't give in to thoughts and doubts,
That might make others cry.

For you are hungry like that cat,
To stretch your legs and run.
And reach for all those dreams you have,
Because that's all the fun.

You see my friend there are in Life,
Few who have your speed.
They mix in groups to give them strength,
But lack those gifts they need.

It is a fact that life is hard,
And there is never rest.
For cats like you who see your vision,
Won't stop for second best.

So run that race despite the thoughts,
That others might succeed.
In taking all you have achieved,
Because they're full of greed.

Cont/

If once you rest and catch your breath,
Then leave them to those spoils.
For in the wisdom you possess,
Are dreams and greater toils.

For as they feast on that gazelle,
Walk away with pride,
If you have helped to feed those who,
Would wish to be on your side.

And raise your head and look beyond,
The sun is setting low.
Those fields are full of herds for you;
So have another go!

Chimpanzee Jamboree

If you ever watch a Chimpanzee,

In the jungle, climb a tree,

You'll know that they are not alone,

With their mates, they're right at home.

In the branches swinging high,

Always looking out to try,

Any games that'll entertain,

Thoughts on which, their minds will train.

Fruitful games of hide and seek,

With fun-filled faces full of cheek,

Their larks are always noisy games,

That brings them joy, which no one blames.

There's always something they can do,

Whilst foraging out some place new,

The Chimpanzee explores its home,

And never wonders off alone.

They roam and make such a fuss,

'Cause Chimpanzees are just like us,

Going ape with Chimps who hang,

And move around in their gang.

Chimpanzees are really creatures,

Who have, to us, our basic features,

So next time when you see his face,

Have a smile and make some space.

For Chimps are mostly born to see,

That happiness is something free,

Imagine being a Chimpanzee,

Living in a virtual Jamboree!

Colleen the Crow

Intent on claiming she has a rightful ambivalence,
As she struts around with a flagrant nonchalance.
That goes to show what underscores a calamity,
But Colleen the Crow displays a sense of vanity.

Looking down her sharp beak in such contempt,
For the weaker fowl from whom she is exempt,
Parading up and down the parapets of society,
She claims a superior intellect as her propriety.

Focused with a beady eye, she will never blink it,
Whilst she seeks to find any form of shiny trinket.
Forever wanting to claim those hidden treasures,
Colleen seems to us, to pursue worldly pleasures.

You will often see her squabbling over any tit-bits,
Her behaviour proclaims a pride she never inhibits.
Where other birds always have a purpose to fulfill,
Colleen appears to act against others with bad will.

Where the pecking order is based on her squawks,
And she flouts that position in the way she walks.
But what does Colleen honestly have to crow about?
It's her actions that confirm all we wish to know about.

Cyril the Squirrel

Cyril the Squirrel is a very cheeky chap,
Who spends winter nights taking a nap,
But when the sun's up on a crisp new day,
Cyril likes to go in search of food and to play.

Being cheeky he always seems happy and bright,
Because his face has a smile and his eyes a delight,
For many a day when you'll see him climbing a tree,
Cyril is often busy storing all his food for his tea.

He rushes and darts in a state that will please,
Stuffing his face with all the acorns he sees,
His cheeks get all puffy as he opens wide,
Keeping them safe, but uneaten inside.

Why does Cyril like to do such a thing?
It's mainly because Squirrels can't sing,
They chirp like a bird, it's a peculiar tone,
You will think they left their voices at home!

But chappies like Cyril they're not so absurd,
He's from another country you might have heard,
Because Cyril is so different from Bertie the Red,
Whose forest he's claimed for himself instead!

We are not saying Cyril is not welcome here,
But we do really think that it is quite clear,
Bertie must not stay an endangered chap,
And hope he won't take a permanent nap!

Debra the Zebra

Debra the Zebra, what a sight to behold,
Her stripes running regular in colours so bold,
A horse in pyjamas is a strange sight to see,
As we wonder about how it can be?

Zebras are partial to living in a herd,
Out on the grasslands where they look quite absurd,
With black and white livery, they move in a haze,
As the sun beats down on hot summer days.

They shimmer in contrast to the African plains,
Where the grass is brown and red dust stains,
But in the herd they move in such a blaze,
Of flickering light that tricks our gaze.

Most other animals blend with their home,
Cleverly camouflaged in the land they roam,
So why does the zebra live in a space,
Where definitive stripes look out of place?

Is it because we keep thinking aloud,
That Zebras are different and look so proud?
For the answer, here is an interesting clue,
As to why those separate stripes are in view!

Whilst safely grazing they, proudly depend,
On keeping eyes focused on stripes that defend,
Each will remain with the herd in the wild,
So that's why you don't have to worry my child?

Foxy the Fox

Foxy has a reputation, it seems he can't deny,

As people think him kind of dirty, and often very sly,

But foxes like to feed at night, and can be seen about,

He overturns the bins outside and behaves like such a lout.

His tail is rather bushy, like a bottle-brush,

He uses it to balance well, when he's in a rush,

He climbs up on the fence, and leaps with a bound,

When looking for the food we bin, that is left on the ground.

You must admit he irritates us with his silly games,

And mom gets mad with him 'n calls him many names,

But there is a reason for why we all, think him such a pest,

'Cause foxes have to hunt for food, when it's time for us to
rest.

A fox is nocturnal, so what's that word you say?

It means that he's up all night, and sleeps in the day.

We never see the baby cubs, he's helping mom to raise,

Tucked away, safe and sound, in the home where he stays.

Think of foxes as no different, really, to you or me,

'Cause then you will be happier, to let them roam free,

Foxes hunt in our streets, and that's why it's such a pity,

They are forced to move closer to us, where we live in a city.

But Foxy is not such a nuisance, as we often think,

'Cause when he's searching out the bins, that really stink,

He'll find a rat, or other critters, that spread a lot of disease,

So I would say that foxes should, be welcome where they
please!

Feisal the Ferret

Feisal the Ferret will be found on the farm,
If ferreting for food as the fowls cry an alarm,
When the farmer is feisty and filled with rage,
Feisal had better find another farm to engage.

'Cause Ferrets like Feisal can fit through a fence,
Which the farmer finds harder to form a defense,
Where Ferrets such as Feisal are slender in form,
The fowl will be mostly, found food for the norm.

'Cause Ferrets like Feisal can formerly find ways,
To ferret through fences, he will find like a maze,
Ferrets are clever and remain forever un-phased,
For Feisal disregards any fences that are raised.

You see Ferrets are likely to forage for their food,
On farms where the fowls are fattened to brood,
For he forsakes fear, when fortuitously forgetful,
Which Feisal the Ferret will forever find regretful.

Because Ferrets are vermin to a farmer who finds,
If his farmyard has been victim to familiar minds,
For Ferrets are fixated when ferreting for the
tasty,
And oftentimes they're found wanting when hasty.

But to a Ferret like Feisal who is due firstly to fail,
It's the system that favours those likely to prevail,
For a Ferret like Feisal it's a fact that they will fall,
When Feisal attempts to climb an unfamiliar wall.

Gerry the Giraffe

Oh isn't it just a laugh,

To see Gerry, the Giraffe,

Stick his head above the trees,

Where he can smell that southern breeze.

You wonder why his neck's so long,

And why his body looks so wrong,

His head is weird it looks so daft.

You'd think he'd catch a windy draft.

He has big eyes that see a mile,

And long eye lashes to make you smile,

So when he sticks out his neck,

You have to say, what the heck?

His lips are made to reach green leaves,

That no one else on earth achieves.

He eats those shoots so crisp and young,

By sticking out his silly tongue.

His legs so long it makes you think,

How on earth can he take a drink?

But drink he does when doing the splits,

And has us rolling with giggling fits.

He's rather odd you'd have to say,

But truth be told he's built that way,

'Cause different means he has the slant,

When eating food that others can't.

Daphne the Deer

Daphne the Deer likes to spend her time grazing,
Out on the glen, where she looks so amazing,
Feeding in herds that is her family affair,
Daphne is happy to forage and share.

'Cause Deer's are vegan and eat plants and grass,
Which is often so plentiful and never too sparse,
You see, Daphne will never have to compete,
For food which she often requires to eat.

The reason why Daphne seems not to be hurried,
Is mostly because she is never too worried,
Her sensitive hearing alert to the danger,
Of anyone she deems likely a stranger.

But Deers like Daphe have learnt not to scurry,
When faced by a threat she is off in a flurry,
Oftentimes whilst she is prancing around,
Her tail will be flickering without a sound.

You see, Deers have learnt to warn one another,
By using their tails as a signal to each other,
They lift them up high and flicker them fast,
As often as is deemed the alarm will last.

Her ears twitching as she scents with her nose,
Daphne looks regal when stood in that pose,
Deers in many ways are lucky and grateful,
She lives a life where no one is hateful.

'Cause Deers like Daphe are a part of a brand,
In which she will live off the fat of the land,
With a status that gives her royal decree,
Daphne is protected, happy and free.

Elgin the Elephant

Elgin the Elephant is ever so strong,
His funny old nose is huge and long,
No matter what, other people may say,
It never ever seems to get in his way.

You might just say, that seems strange,
But Elephant's today, have had to change,
Because over time, their noses grew,
So they learned to to use it for something new.

His nose is now formed to eat and to prod,
Even though this seems so wonderf'ly odd,
He eats with his nose, is that what you say?
Yes! It seems that he is born that way!

An Elephant can use his nose in many ways,
One of which is when he's learning to graze,
He reaches down and grasps with his nose,
The grasses and leaves, which he has chose.

How he can eat, it is quite easy to understand!
'Cause the tip of his trunk is formed like a hand,
He opens his mouth, where his nose now lingers,
Stuffing food in his mouth with those fingers.

Elephants need water, which makes you think,
How is it possible for Elgin to drink?
With his nose in the water he sniffs and draws,
Using it like giant milk-shake straws.

Harry the Hare

What does Harry the Hare have to hear to be here?
It is hearing what is heard with a large hairy ear,
When out in the fields where a Hare has to hear,
The hearing of Hares has helped him stay here.

If a Hare has hairy ears too large to be an ear,
Without those two ears Harry could not hear!
A Hare's hair is soft and here's why he's hairy,
'Cause Harry needs his soft hair light and airy.

So how does a Hare's ears help him to hear?
Harry hears when he turns them here and there,
Because if those ears stick out there and here,
Harry can hear what a Hare needs to hear!

A Hares life is hard and can be quite hairy,
When things that Hares hear are often scary!
But Harry is here because his hearing will hear,
Any sound that Hares ears would likely fear!

Because Hares stick together as a family there,
Hairy whiskers twitching as they smell the air,
And Harry the Hare will so often lend an ear,
To those Hares in his family he holds quite dear!

They hare around when they hear what they hear,
'Cause a Hare won't dare to ignore what is there,
But Harry the Hare will run out of breath there,
After hopping away by the breadth of a hair!

Hares have this hearing so that they will hear,
Any sound that could happen to harm a Hare!
But no one will ever hurt a hair on this Hare,
'Cause the hairs on his head are Harry's hair!

Hilda the Hedgehog

Hilda the Hedgehog has ants in her pants,
Because she is off to the Hedgehog dance,
Where Hilda is going you don't have to ask,
She won't stop for anyone, unless in a mask.

Because bumping into Hilda at the local ball,
One might not be tempted to remember it all,
It is where Hedgehogs go to meet and greet,
And when there's good food they like to eat.

Her favourite snacks are a squiggly worm,
Which Hedgehogs eat, and make us squirm,
But Hilda the Hedgehog likes those things,
And eat she does, these bugs with wings,

She will shuffle along while eating them all,
And shnuffles them up as fast as they crawl,
Scurrying through hedgerows is a simple thing,
For Hedgehogs whose coats stop any oting.

When dancing with Hedgehogs it's quite a dare,
'Cause a dance with a Hedgehog is a prickly affair,
Where the dancers like to hold on 'specially tight,
'Cause a partner will have a problem with sight.

So it's better to side-step and keep quite aware,
That a Hedgehog two-step might seem quite rare,
But for Hedgehogs it seems it's not so bizarre,
You see Hilda the Hedgehog can't see that far.

Hippy the Hippo

Hippy the Hippo thinks she's so cool,
Hanging around in that Hippo pool,
How is it she gets to wallow all day,
Down in the water to gossip and play?

The reason she's popular is because of her fame,
It's not that she's hip like her name might explain,
She gets the attention of all in her pod,
When shouting the loudest and getting the nod.

But why do the others who frolic and splash,
Listen to who she is wanting to bash,
And arguing over just who is allowed,
To swim in the pool and hang with the crowd?

Hippos are just like the people we know,
They squabble and posture and put on a show,
To justify why they should have a say,
On who is included among those who can stay.

But there is a reason she's having such fun,
Deep in the pool and out of the sun,
It's because her skin can't tolerate the heat,
And the pool is simply a welcome retreat.

So next time you see Hippy in the pool,
Remember it's 'cause she's trying to keep cool,
Hiding her weakness and making amends,
And not simply trying to bully her friends!

Monkey Business

Charlie is always up to pranks,
Which is why he's in the naughty ranks,
Hanging out, in the park,
With his friends, after dark,
Swinging through the trees he goes,
Up to what mischief, goodness knows?
But Charlie is no different to,
The kids from school that we once knew,
The only difference it would seem,
Is that Charlie has a different dream,
And life is filled with thoughts of where,
Monkey's play without a care.
'Cause life today has somehow changed,
From those days when we once ranged,
In a troop through forest groves,
In pursuit of fun in droves,
For monkeys play for want of joy,
And live without a fear, my boy!

So why do parents fuss and scold,
Monkeys that aren't very old?
It's just because they're told to fear,
The things that might harm you dear!
But truth be told, it's in their mind,
Because of things that you might find.
So if your Mom should have a fit,
And goes bananas when you won't sit,
To listen when she calls you in,
Try not making some noisy din,
'Cause Moms are naturally scared,

Cont/

Of things that friends of yours have dared.
The mother has, an instinct for trouble,
And that is why they keep seeing double,
'Cause a mother knows when to stress,
When her kids are getting in a mess,
In that jungle there is no finesse,
When kids get up to monkey business!

Ollie the Otter

Ollie the Otter is an inordinate creature,
Out in the waves while he fishes for lunch,
It's a lark for an Otter whose catch will feature,
Chasing mackerel tightly packed in a bunch.

But Ollie is never a misbehaved Otter,
Because he will never take out more than his fill,
You see Ollie is having fun and is no shameless rotter,
For him it's a game and the chase is a thrill.

He uses his tail to plunge deep into the ocean,
Which helps him speed, at a pace through the shoal,
Because Ollie the Otter looks like a flurry of motion,
And he won't stop 'till he's has secured his goal.

His eyes open wide he's hunting tasty morsels,
And his coat is so smooth and slick with natural oil,
Avoiding those he fears by the size of their dorsals.
Because for Ollie the Otter catching fish is no toil,

Keeping his prey, firmly grasped in his claws,
Ollie the Otter now heads back for some air,
He likes chewing away with his whiskered jaws
He eats whilst floating laid-back without a care.

He really does look a slap-happy fellow,
That reminds us of that wide grin on his face,
That's 'cause Ollie knows the secrets to be mellow,
Whilst living a life well and always finishing the race.

Percy the Peacock

Percy the Peacock is out, proud and loud.
And doesn't mind standing out in a crowd,
With a full rainbow hue of feathers in view,
Percy reminds us of someone we knew.

Percy the Peacock has a voice that's so shrill,
It is hard to contain what a klaxon could fulfil,
Abrupt and invasive this smacks us as foul,
But Percy is only having a long-awaited howl!

Peacocks like Percy were once stripped bare,
Their souls now featherless, for people to stare,
But long-sought protections, are now permitted,
And the mistakes of the past are gladly admitted.

Percy the Peacock once more suitably regaled,
Is happy to stand and shout out what had failed,
His iridescent displays are now eagerly awaited,
By a gathering of his hens never 'quite' satiated.

The lesson for Percy the Peacock will be borne,
By a society of doubters in whom love is forlorn,
For when a community is vibrant and iridescent,
It helps to provide a place that is effervescent.

'Cause Percy was once hunted into submission,
So you have to realise that his global ambition,
Is to finally stand rewarded without fear nor favour,
And shout from the hilltops with 'nerry a waiver!

Phil the Pheasant

Phil the Pheasant looks like a fairly plucky fellow,
Whose feathers are refined in a fiercely bold yellow,
Faced with a turquoise fiesta of the finest display,
Featured with a myriad in a freckle-feathered array.

Phil the pheasant cuts a fastidiously formed figure,
His famously fitting formula flouts a profile of vigour
Framed from fertile jasper forests in a fanciful facade,
He flaunts with futile fervour with furtive disregard.

Phil the Pheasant is fondly found in forceful forays,
Foraging phenomenally in fabulously fruitful ways,
With a favourable full flight of finely fettled feathers,
We find him fluttering in fields of fragrant heathers.

For Phil the Pheasant's finery forms a feasible feast,
Fortuitously camouflaged from any frenzied beast,
A fancifully fattened pheasant will formerly appeal,
When falling fowl to a flavourful fantastical meal.

Phil the Pheasant's formidable font of rainbow hues,
Will forever have to fight for his flamboyant dues,
'Cause Phil has a familiarity found forever wanting,
When the pheasant plucker's son is fond of hunting.

Sally the Sable

The Sable is an animal so majestically displayed,
His great curved horns in profile splendidly arrayed,
With dark tanned hide standing in contrast to the trees,
As if to say to other beasts, come on, try me if you please!

The Sable is an antelope, so beautifully sublime,
When looking at how few are left it is an awful crime,
Because it is unfortunate, for The Sable, his lovely horn,
Is something that, if he could, he would wish to not be born!

The Sable is true evidence to the great foundation,
Handsome symbol of a time when nature ruled creation
But surely no one has the right to want horns dis-approved,
So why would you wish to have those lovely horns removed?

The Sable had few enemies during a place in history,
Before the world was confused by a strange new mystery,
It was a time when nature ruled and animals were very dear,
When creatures roamed the land they owned without any fear!

The Sable so magnificent, who would wish them harm,
Surviving within a garden world, where they lived so calm,
But then Man came and stamped their mark on the very land,
Upon which the animals thrived, so the balance could not
stand!

The Sable has few predators except for trophy killers,
Paying to shoot them with a gun like some crazy thrillers,
Because their beauty stands a testimony to creative change,
The Sable is a symbol of the African land on which they range!

Walter the Weasel

Walter the Weasel is one of our wayward friends,
Spending time saying sorry and making amends,
He scurries around leaving havoc and disaster,
Entering the fray quickly and leaving even faster.

Walter will argue with a self-determined surety,
Based on the guise of self-proclaimed maturity,
Keenly aware that he has been graced with a gift,
Walter the Weasel displays some peculiar grift!

Friends like Walter need to learn lowly prudence,
But are schooled in the art of risk with due-diligence,
After all he is a lowly creature of nocturnal habit,
Entering the domain down the 'Hole of a Rabbit'

Because Walter the Weasel is always happy to play,
Provided your games are not left in total disarray,
You see Weasels have been given some short thrift,
When reputations are squandered and egos are miffed!

Weasels can be found in lairs in and around a city,
Where they tend to hibernate for a winter of self-pity,
But as soon as spring has returned to the country,

They are soon back to their ways in blatant effrontery.

Cont/

As a Weasels pointy face looks a bit like a clown,
So don't be surprised if Walter lets you down,
Just remember to think why he behaves this way,
Which shows that he is only a friend for a day.

'Cause a Weasel is really what their names sound,
And rarely are willing to stand and hold their ground,
With argumentative fervour sure to catch your breath,
Weasels like Walter are likely to lawyer you to death.

Wendy the Warthog

When will Wendy Warthog go?
To find some mud in which to wallow,
It's usually when the sun is bright,
'Cause lions sleep mostly by day, not night.
She snorts and fusses her little brood,
Making noises that seem rather rude,
'Cause warthogs live in darkened burrows,
Why you say? Well no one knows!
But down below they can't watch telly,
And truth be told, it's rather smelly.
So when you think she's had enough,
She'll sound displeased and get the huff,
But once she's checked the coast is clear,
They're up and out, into the glare,
With tails raised high they trot in time,
Down to see where the mud's sublime,
With trotters first they test the mud,
Then leap right in with cheerful thud,
And rolling round with wild delight,
They look so happy, just what a sight!
All that oozing mud on their skin,
No wonder their faces have such a grin!
Amidst all the revelry the Mom is alert,
For unwanted lions who don't like the dirt,
For even a lion can't sleep for long,
When grumbling tummies are singing a song.
She listens and hears if the lion's approach,
Scurrying home with kids,
'Cause she's no slow coach!

Thank you to all those people who have inspired my poems, providing a humourous interlude between writing my novels and completing my recent dissertation on Spirituality.

Come to think of it, these poems were in fact created whilst looking upon our human family, and recognising many spiritual characteristics that advanced my understanding of people, by equating them to wild animals. Concluding this anthology has left me thinking we have a lot more in common with our animal family; than the difference our physicality may suggest.

Acknowledgements to © LifeZone Publishing for graphics.

Printed in Great Britain
by Amazon

41929528R00029